OCT -- 2022

KILGORE MEMORIAL LIBRARY
520 North Nebraska Avenue
York, NE 68467
(402) 363-2620

CRISIS IN UKRAINE

NATO

Tyler Gieseke

Abdo & Daughters
MIDDLE GRADE NONFICTION
An imprint of Abdo Publishing
abdobooks.com

ABDOBOOKS.COM

Published by Abdo Publishing, a division of ABDO, PO Box 398166, Minneapolis, Minnesota 55439. Copyright © 2023 by Abdo Consulting Group, Inc. International copyrights reserved in all countries. No part of this book may be reproduced in any form without written permission from the publisher. Abdo & Daughters™ is a trademark and logo of Abdo Publishing.

Printed in the United States of America, North Mankato, Minnesota.
052022
092022

Editor: Bridget O'Brien

Series Designer: Laura Graphenteen

Cover Photographs: Marion S. Trikosko/photographer/Library of Congress (left); Shutterstock Images

Interior Photographs: ALFRED/SIPA/AP Images, pp. 34-35; Gerald Herbert/AP Images, p. 49; Harry Todd/Stringer/Getty Images, pp. 10-11; Keystone/Stringer/Getty Images, p. 29; Keystone-France/Contributor/Getty Images, pp. 14-15, 18-19; Liu Heung Shing/AP Images, p. 37; Shutterstock Images, pp. 4-5, 6, 7, 9, 17, 20-21, 23, 24-25, 28, 30-31, 33, 38, 40-41, 43, 44-45, 46-47, 48, 51, 55, 56-57, 59; STR/AP Images, pp. 26-27; Uncredited/Associated Press/AP Images, pp. 13, 52-53; Visar Kryeziu/AP Images, p. 8; Werner Kreusch/AP Images, p. 22

Design Elements: Shutterstock Images

LIBRARY OF CONGRESS CONTROL NUMBER: 2022934956

PUBLISHER'S CATALOGING-IN-PUBLICATION DATA

Names: Gieseke, Tyler, author.

Title: NATO / by Tyler Gieseke

Description: Minneapolis, Minnesota : ABDO Publishing, 2023 | Series: Crisis in Ukraine | Includes online resources and index.

Identifiers: ISBN 9781532199127 (lib. bdg.) | ISBN 9781098273101 (ebook)

Subjects: LCSH: North Atlantic Treaty Organization--Juvenile literature. | North Atlantic Treaty Organization--Armed Forces--Juvenile literature. | Security, International--Juvenile literature. | Military readiness--Juvenile literature.

Classification: DDC 341.24--dc23

TABLE OF CONTENTS

CHOOSING SIDES. 5
ORIGINS 11
TAKING ROOT. 15
THE WARSAW PACT 19
DÉTENTE. 25
TWO TRACKS 31
THE END OF THE COLD WAR 35
INTO THE 21ST CENTURY. 41
CRISIS IN UKRAINE 47
TO BE OR NOT TO BE . . . INVOLVED 53
SUPPORT FROM A DISTANCE 57
TIMELINE OF NATO 60

Glossary 62
Online Resources 63
Index 64

President Petro Poroshenko of Ukraine, *center*, addresses members of parliament in September 2017.

CHAPTER ONE

CHOOSING SIDES

In June 2017, the Eastern European country of Ukraine decided it would ally itself with Western European countries and democratic values. It was a bold move for one of the largest former members of the Union of Soviet Socialist Republics (USSR). The USSR was a union that was famously communist and anti-West. Ukraine is also a neighbor to Russia. Russia dominated the USSR as a global superpower during the Cold War.

The Ukrainian parliament passed a law in June 2017 that the country would aim to qualify for membership in the North Atlantic Treaty Organization (NATO). A majority of 276 members of parliament out of 450 voted for the law. For over 60 years, NATO had represented Western military power, capitalism, and

Poroshenko speaks in 2017 in Kyiv, Ukraine.

democracy. NATO had gone head-to-head with Eastern communist countries during the forty years of the Cold War. Now, one of communism's former strongholds was switching sides.

"Ukraine has clearly defined its political future and its future in the sphere of security," Ukrainian president Petro Poroshenko said of the law. "Today we clearly stated that we would begin a discussion about a membership action plan." Two years later, the goal of earning NATO membership became an amendment to Ukraine's constitution.

The Russians were not happy with the news. Russian officials said Ukraine's aspirations to join NATO would spark tensions in Europe. Russia had spoken out against Eastern European countries becoming NATO members for years. In 2022, Ukraine's discussions with NATO partly led to a Russian invasion of the country in February.

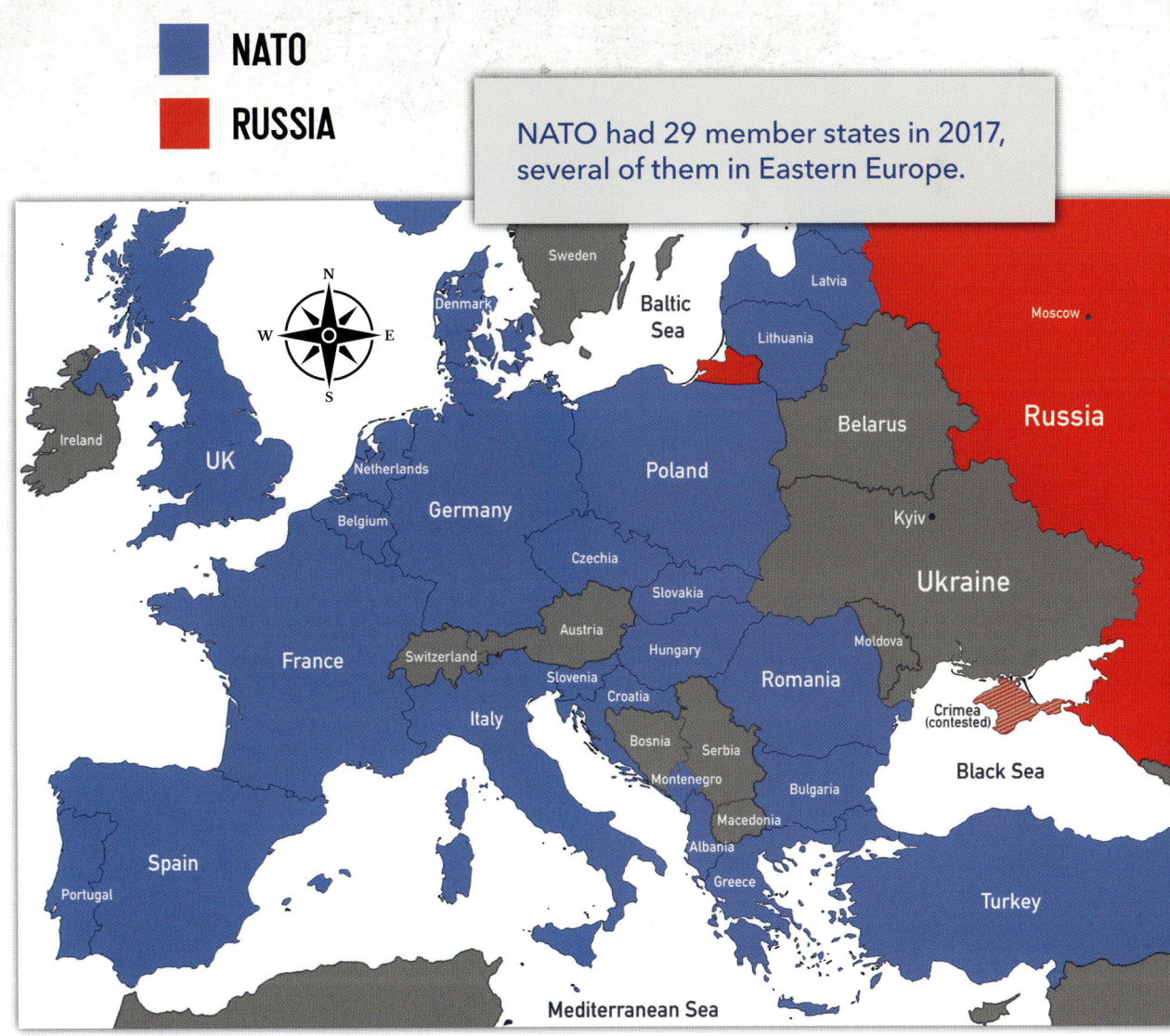

NATO had 29 member states in 2017, several of them in Eastern Europe.

The Ukraine crisis posed a challenge for NATO. The organization was initially designed to halt Soviet expansion in Europe after World War II. At the time, NATO was a defensive pact. That had changed in the decades since.

NATO had taken a more active role in international crises. This was especially true following the end of the Cold War in the late 1980s. NATO would periodically take targeted military action to end conflicts or protect civilians from inhumane treatment.

The organization found itself at the center of a debate during the Ukraine crisis in 2022. How much and what kind of involvement should it have in the war? Ukraine was a friend to NATO. But it was not a member. To answer the question, the North Atlantic Treaty Organization would have to consider its own past.

Some NATO military forces remain in unstable regions for years.

Polish soldiers on patrol as part of a NATO mission in 2021

When World War II ended in Europe, people had to live with damaged or destroyed buildings.

CHAPTER TWO

ORIGINS

The North Atlantic Treaty Organization was formed in the aftermath of World War II. It was a reaction to an unstable Europe and encroaching forces from the East. World War II ended after almost six years of conflict in Europe on May 8, 1945.

There was finally peace. But the continent had paid a high price to achieve it. More than 30 million of its people had died. Many cities were left sorely damaged. Europe was free, but it was broken and relatively vulnerable.

At the same time, the USSR (or Soviet Union) was growing its political and military control in Eastern Europe. The USSR was a union of communist countries dominated by Russia. The Soviet Union had played a key role in ending World War II in Europe.

Following the war, communist leaders began to gain control in Eastern European countries on the USSR's borders. These included Poland, Hungary, Romania, and Bulgaria. The communist leaders were loyal to the USSR.

The advance of Soviet control concerned many Western European countries. They believed in free markets where people could work, buy, and sell how they wanted. The countries of the USSR were communist. This meant the government determined how goods and services were made and sold. Western Europe worried that the Soviets would continue to expand.

Twelve countries signed the North Atlantic Treaty in Washington, DC, on April 4, 1949. From Europe there was Belgium, Denmark, France, Iceland, Italy, Luxembourg, the Netherlands, Norway, Portugal, and the United Kingdom. From North America there was the United States (US) and Canada.

The treaty had three primary goals. First, it was meant to strengthen Europe while it continued to rebuild after World War II. Second, the treaty would serve as protection from Soviet forces. Third, the treaty would promote cooperation among European nations. It would prevent the return of European nationalism, which had been a factor in the start of World War II. The North Atlantic Treaty Organization was born.

A defining part of the treaty was collective defense. This idea meant that if one of the member countries was attacked by an outside force, all NATO countries would help defend.

According to Article 5 of the treaty, "an armed attack against one or more of [the members] . . . shall be considered an attack against them all." This would remain a NATO focus until the fall of the USSR 40 years later.

Belgian prime minister Paul-Henri Spaak (*bottom center*) is the first to sign the North Atlantic Treaty. US president Harry Truman sits just to the right of the center microphones.

The Supreme Headquarters Allied Powers Europe in October 1959

CHAPTER THREE
TAKING ROOT

After the North Atlantic Treaty was signed, member countries put together political structures. These would help them carry out the treaty. The organization's first headquarters was established in London, England, in 1949. In 1952, it moved to Paris, France, where it would remain for over a decade. Leaders named it the Supreme Headquarters Allied Powers Europe (SHAPE). SHAPE was a central location where officials of the member countries could meet and make decisions.

Leadership would coordinate the diverse members and their military units. The first supreme allied commander Europe (SACEUR) was US military general Dwight D. Eisenhower. Eisenhower had played an influential role during World War II.

The SACEUR position was created in 1950. It would oversee military operations and obtain forces from member countries. The chief civilian position, secretary general, was established in 1952. The secretary general would lead NATO's decision-making process and administration. Lord Hastings Lionel Ismay was the first to have this job. He was a United Kingdom official.

As NATO's structure grew, so did wider European interest in the organization. Greece and Turkey joined NATO in 1952, followed by West Germany in 1955. The treaty offered membership to "any other European state in a position to further the principles of this Treaty and to contribute to the security of the North Atlantic area." All current members had to agree to admit a new member nation. New members had to contribute to collective defense if necessary.

NATO continued to build its defense policies. In the mid-1950s, NATO adopted the massive retaliation doctrine. This meant a nuclear attack on a NATO country would be answered with strong nuclear force.

The massive retaliation doctrine was designed to

DWIGHT D. EISENHOWER

Dwight D. "Ike" Eisenhower was born in Texas in 1890 and raised in Kansas. He joined the army and led US forces at the pivotal D-Day battle in 1944. After helping organize NATO, Ike served as US president for two terms, from 1953 to 1961.

Eisenhower sits at his desk at SHAPE in January 1952.

prevent a nuclear attack from Soviet forces. If the USSR expected NATO to react with nuclear force, it would be less likely to launch the first nuclear attack.

In a few short years, NATO had grown. It went from a signed piece of paper to a 15-country organization with a leadership structure and a policy of defense against communist nuclear power. This period of widespread political and diplomatic maneuvers pitting East against West was known as the Cold War. The war was considered "cold" because there was no direct fighting between the opposing sides. Yet, each party threatened the other. When one side made an advance, the other side would respond with a similar move. The formation of NATO was one such advance. The USSR would quickly match NATO with its own treaty.

The Warsaw Pact is signed by Polish prime minister Jozef Cyrankiewicz.

CHAPTER FOUR

THE WARSAW PACT

A new collective defense treaty was signed in Warsaw, Poland, on May 14, 1955. This counterpoint to the North Atlantic Treaty was known as the Warsaw Pact. The USSR dominated the pact. It was partly a response to West Germany joining NATO. It would also help solidify the Cold War opposition between the Eastern and Western powers.

The members of the Warsaw Pact were the USSR, Poland, East Germany, Czechoslovakia, Hungary, Romania, Bulgaria, and Albania. They agreed to defend each other if one of the member countries was attacked.

A Soviet commander in chief led Warsaw Pact forces. The USSR also kept its own forces in the member nations. The approximately 500,000 Warsaw Pact soldiers included

Russians, Bulgarians, Poles, and Hungarians. Romania, Albania, and East Germany declined to supply military forces.

Not all members of the Warsaw Pact were happy with the agreement. In 1956, Hungary's government wanted to leave the pact. The government also wanted USSR forces to leave Hungary. The country fought back against the USSR. Poland also resisted Soviet control that year.

In each case, Warsaw Pact forces stopped the uprisings. The member countries were already under heavy communist influence. Plus, the Warsaw Pact strengthened USSR control over them.

Europe was divided between NATO countries in the West and Warsaw Pact countries in the East. Each group felt protected from the other because of the collective agreements. The situation was uneasy but stable. Neither side would directly attack the other.

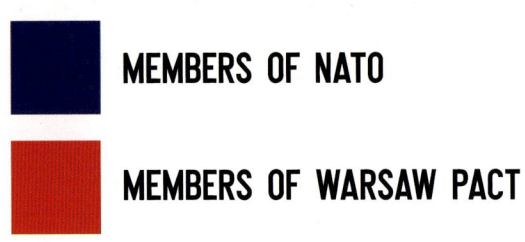

West Berlin children try to see over the wall and into East Berlin in August 1961.

A 1957 NATO conference showed that members were more interested in political rather than military action. Eisenhower gave a speech at the conference. He was now president of the United States.

He said NATO was a "military shield" that should be kept "so long as there is any menace to the freedom of the Western nations. . . . We have the collective power to defend and spread . . . freedom. Freedom has not failed us; surely we shall not fail freedom." The idea that NATO was a "shield" against aggressive forces highlights that the organization was meant to prevent military action rather than start it.

The Cold War was deeply entrenched by the end of the decade. A symbol of the political division of the time was the Berlin Wall. The USSR built the wall in 1961 to separate West Berlin and East Berlin. It was made of concrete and barbed wire. The Berlin Wall became a physical reminder of the hostility between Eastern and Western powers.

A policeman patrols on the West Berlin side of the wall while builders from East Berlin add layers of bricks in October 1961.

US president John F. Kennedy (*left*) and US general Lauris Norstad (*right*), NATO's supreme commander, at SHAPE

CHAPTER FIVE

DÉTENTE

The power-grabbing and defensive postures of the post-World War II era softened in the 1960s. East and West both had collective defense structures, and the two powers had laid claim to most of Europe. Emphasis switched from being prepared for possible war to developing friendlier relations between the groups. New, more flexible military policies were introduced.

US president John F. Kennedy's administration adopted a "flexible response" approach in the early 1960s. This replaced the earlier doctrine of massive retaliation against Soviet Union aggression.

The new policy allowed for reactions that were less extreme than heavy nuclear counterattacks. The administration believed this

The Belgium SHAPE opens in March 1967 with the raising of flags.

would lower tensions around Soviet confrontations. The move also showed the gradual decrease of tensions at the time.

Other countries were also reconsidering military policies. France announced it would leave NATO's military arm in 1966. French leaders asked that the NATO headquarters be moved outside the country. By October 1967, the new SHAPE was in Brussels, Belgium.

France's decision to exit military operations tested NATO's cohesion. People worried other member countries might change their involvement as well.

There was also concern about the organization's continued existence. Member countries would be allowed to leave the agreement starting in 1969. It seemed NATO was becoming less relevant almost two decades after its start.

But by the end of 1967, a bigger purpose was forming for NATO. This new role was called détente. It would go beyond defending against Eastern powers. It would embrace building relationships with them and other countries.

A December paper known as the Harmel Report laid the groundwork for détente. The report was delivered by Belgium's minister of foreign affairs, Pierre Harmel. In it, Harmel said that "military security and a policy of détente are not contradictory but complementary. . . The way to peace and stability in Europe rests in particular on the use of the Alliance constructively in the interest of détente." In

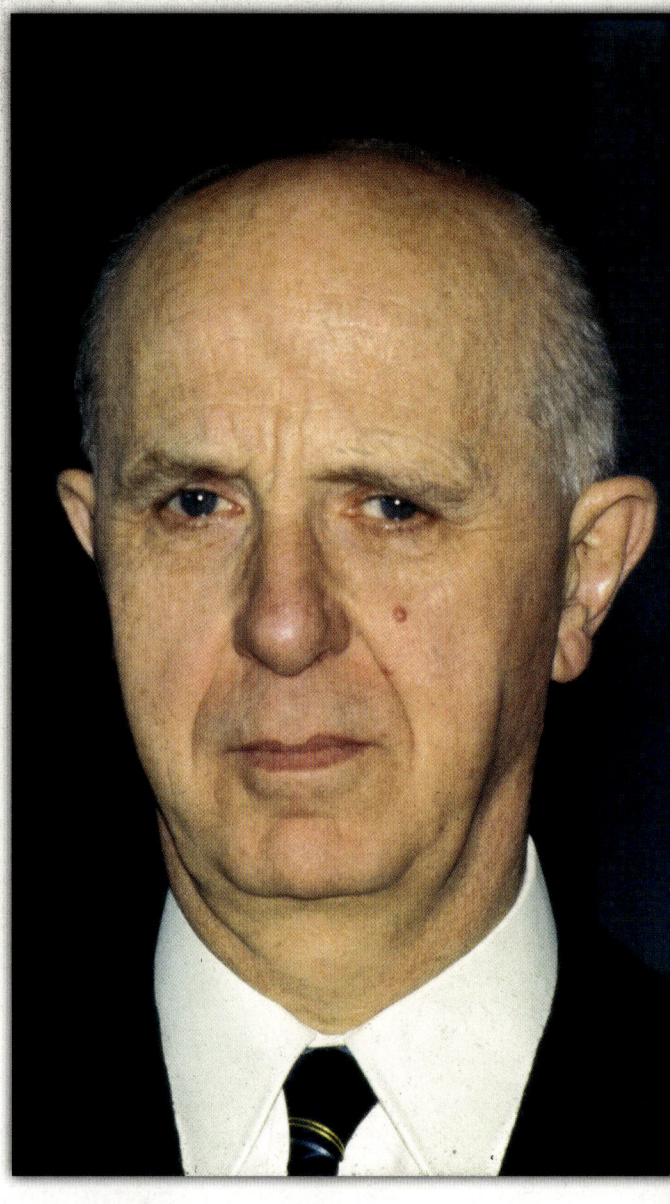

Pierre Harmel served in various Belgian political roles during his life.

a new European political landscape, a commitment to diplomacy would be NATO's way forward.

The Soviet Union also produced a new political doctrine during this period. It was called the Brezhnev Doctrine, after communist leader Leonid Brezhnev. The doctrine meant the Soviet Union would use force to maintain communist control in its satellite states.

A 1968 announcement of the policy said socialist countries should make their own choices. But it also said that "none of [the countries'] decisions should damage either socialism in their country or the fundamental interests of other socialist countries." The policy was carried out that year. Soviet troops suppressed a reform movement in Czechoslovakia known as the Prague Spring.

Leonid Brezhnev laughs in Paris in June 1973.

A Soviet tank and soldiers rest in Afghanistan in 1980 following the first entry of Soviet forces in 1979.

CHAPTER SIX

TWO TRACKS

Détente came to an end in the late 1970s. The USSR sent forces to Afghanistan in 1979 to support a communist government there. This angered the democratic West. The Soviets also stationed intermediate-range missiles in Europe, which threatened the Western states there. NATO decided to use both force and diplomacy in a "dual track" response. By the close of the 1980s, there were hints that the Cold War was nearing its end.

Politically left military leaders took over Afghanistan in 1978. The new socialist parties that dominated grew close with the Soviet Union. But much of the Muslim Afghan population was against communism. Islamic groups fought back against the socialist government.

The Soviet Union took control on December 24, 1979, with 30,000 troops. It hoped to stabilize communist rule in Afghanistan. The United States wanted to stop any spread of communist influence. It supported the Islamic rebels. These aggressive moves put an end to détente.

A second development against détente was the USSR's placement of more than 200 SS-20 Saber ballistic missiles in Europe. These weapons posed a direct threat to Western European countries. They had a range of about 3,100 miles (5,000 km). The situation made further positive relationships between East and West difficult.

NATO countries reacted to the Soviets with a two-pronged or "dual track" approach. The first track of the plan was military. The West announced it would station Pershing II missiles in Europe beginning in 1983. This would show the

CUBAN MISSILE CRISIS

There were other Cold War-era missile disputes. In 1962, the USSR began building nuclear missiles in Cuba. The US had missiles in Turkey. President Kennedy set up a naval blockade of Cuba in October and threatened to attack the USSR if the project continued. Soviet premier Nikita Khrushchev agreed to remove the missiles. And, Kennedy agreed to take the missiles out of Turkey. The crisis is understood as the closest the world has come to nuclear war.

A Pershing II missile in West Germany

Soviets that the Western countries could respond with nuclear force if necessary. The second track was diplomatic. NATO officials would continue to seek agreements with Soviet leaders to reduce arms.

Unable to come to an arms agreement, NATO began to deploy Pershing II missiles in 1983. But talks between Western and Eastern powers continued. In 1985, Mikhail Gorbachev rose to power as the Soviet premier. He was committed to reform. This brought new hope to negotiations between East and West.

The United States and the USSR signed the Intermediate-Range Nuclear Forces Treaty in 1987. Gorbachev and US president Ronald Reagan agreed to remove missiles that could travel an intermediate distance. This distance was approximately 310 to 3,420 miles (500–5,500 km). The treaty was an important move toward peace. Many thought it meant the Cold War could soon end.

West Berliners work to destroy the Berlin Wall in November 1989.

CHAPTER SEVEN

THE END OF THE COLD WAR

The Cold War was indeed coming to an end. Toward the end of the 1980s, the Soviet Union's influence in the East began to fade. The USSR's economy was just one-third that of the United States. The Soviets were spending heavily on military projects. This depleted an already struggling economy. The military focus soon dwindled with Gorbachev in charge. So did Soviet control of the East.

In East Germany, people called for reform and a relaxation of the police state. Activists wanted a more liberal socialism "with a human face." The communist leadership of East Germany asked Gorbachev for help keeping control.

But the Soviet premier decided not to interfere. This went against the Brezhnev

Doctrine. Like many of the East German people, Gorbachev supported reform.

Gorbachev asked East German leaders to consider change. But they delayed in implementing it. Soon, the momentum against the communist rulers appeared to be too strong.

East German leaders faced growing opposition from reformers. They allowed travel out of East Berlin starting November 9, 1989. That day, millions of people crossed through the Berlin Wall. Many helped tear it down with hammers, picks, and even bulldozers. The symbol of the Cold War was no more. Would the actual end of the Cold War come with it?

The answer came within the next few years—yes. East and West Germany were reunited on October 3, 1990, more than 40 years after their creation. West Germany absorbed East Germany. It made the new state a NATO member.

"TEAR DOWN THIS WALL"

On June 12, 1987, then US president Ronald Reagan gave a passionate speech near the Berlin Wall. He called for peace and openness in East-West relations, which were beginning to relax under Gorbachev.

Reagan spoke for 26 minutes. About halfway through his speech, he famously said: "Mr. Gorbachev, open this gate! Mr. Gorbachev, tear down this wall!" A little over two years later, Berlin citizens listened. They tore down the wall.

Gorbachev signs documents on the day of his resignation, December 25, 1991.

At the same time, the USSR's hold on its satellite countries continued to weaken. Gorbachev resigned from his post on December 25, 1991. This signaled the end of the USSR. The Warsaw Pact dissolved that year as well. The Cold War was over.

State leaders attend a press conference on March 16, 1999, when Hungary, the Czech Republic, and Poland joined NATO.

NATO had succeeded in protecting its member countries during the Cold War. For a period, it had also served as a diplomatic forum with the Soviets. But now that the Cold War was over, the organization again faced a question of identity.

One of the three founding goals of NATO was obsolete. But two of them remained: to strengthen European organization and promote political cooperation. NATO would focus on these missions in the coming decades.

A key part in building a more politically unified Europe was the Partnership for Peace program formed in 1994. Through this program, nonmember countries could dialogue with NATO, assist with its tasks, and prepare to become full members.

Three former Soviet satellite countries became NATO members in 1999. Poland, the Czech Republic, and Hungary all joined the alliance. This brought the total members to 19. Spain had also joined back in 1982.

SPAIN JOINS NATO

Spain became a NATO member on May 30, 1982, but its acceptance was controversial. Until 1975, Francisco Franco had ruled as dictator of Spain. This form of government ran counter to NATO's democratic ideals. And in 1982, Spanish politics was dominated by the Socialist Workers' Party. NATO countries traditionally supported capitalism rather than socialism.

Early in its membership, Spain declined to join NATO's military arm. But the country agreed to do so in 1996, when Dr. Javier Solana was serving as the first NATO secretary general from Spain.

A NATO soldier directs a crowd in 1999 as the Yugoslav Army prepares to withdraw following the Kosovo conflict.

CHAPTER EIGHT

INTO THE 21ST CENTURY

As NATO neared the turn of the millennium, it produced a strategy document that laid out its new operational approach. The strategy had already taken form during the 1990s. The 1999 Strategic Concept was published in April at a summit in Washington, DC. It redefined NATO's purpose to include targeted military operations.

This broke from the organization's Cold War–era focus on defense. Part 1 was called "The Purpose and Tasks of the Alliance." It said that NATO "not only ensures the defence of its members but contributes to peace and stability in [the North Atlantic] region."

For NATO, contributing to peace might include military action. This was usually after diplomatic options had failed. For example, a civil conflict between Albanians and Serbs in the Kosovo region intensified in the late 1990s. Serbian forces were following an ethnic cleansing policy against the Albanians. The Albanians had begun armed uprisings earlier in the decade to support the independence of the Kosovo state.

After a broken cease-fire agreement, unsuccessful peace talks, and a United Nations arms embargo, NATO began to use force. The organization led a months-long air raid campaign and other attacks in Kosovo. The Serbians withdrew in the summer of 1999. Then, NATO troops entered the region to enforce peace. Targeted military missions such as this would come to define NATO's operations in the twenty-first century.

The next decade saw NATO increasing its reach and influence, both in the North Atlantic region and

LIBYA CRISIS

In the early 2010s, civil unrest against rigid rulers in North Africa and the Middle East became known as the Arab Spring. Many protests were peaceful, but ruler Muammar al-Qaddafi in Libya began killing protestors in February 2011.

The United Nations created a no-fly zone in support of Libyan rebels in March. NATO agreed to command the foreign forces on March 27. NATO forces helped rebels attack Qaddafi's government, and the former ruler was forced from power by the end of the year.

elsewhere. In 2002, the NATO-Russia Council formed. This was a diplomatic platform to promote cooperation in security matters with a former Cold War rival.

The following year, NATO took over responsibility for the International Security Assistance Force (ISAF). The ISAF was a UN-approved multinational force meant to stabilize Afghanistan. After the 9/11 terrorist attacks, the United States and some NATO countries had invaded Afghanistan in 2001. In this instance and others, NATO was branching out beyond its North Atlantic home.

ISAF soldiers stand outside the group's headquarters in Kabul, Afghanistan.

    Contributing to the expansion was a whole host of new members. In 2004, seven European nations became NATO members. These nations were Bulgaria, Estonia, Latvia, Lithuania, Romania, Slovakia, and Slovenia. In 2009, Croatia and Albania were granted membership as well. Their entry brought the total number of countries in the alliance to 28. Membership had more than doubled since the original 12 members signed the North Atlantic Treaty 60 years earlier.

Flags flew at half-mast at NATO headquarters in April 2010 after Polish president Lech Kaczynski, his wife, and Polish officials died in a plane crash.

NATO released another strategic concept in November 2010. The newest approach continued the tasks of collective defense and crisis management. It also included a third: cooperative security. This meant NATO would "engage actively to enhance international security." It could accomplish this by working with other international groups such as the African Union, promoting reductions in arms, and developing new NATO members who shared the alliance's values. NATO had entered the twenty-first century.

NATO secretary general Jens Stoltenberg and Ukrainian president Volodymyr Zelenskyy shake hands at an October 2019 meeting.

CHAPTER NINE

CRISIS IN UKRAINE

NATO's expansion into Eastern Europe in the early twenty-first century was a continuing sore point for Russia. Russia had once dominated as one of the two superpowers during the Cold War. Since Vladimir Putin had become the Russian president in 1999, three former Soviet republics had joined NATO—Estonia, Latvia, and Lithuania. Ukraine was one of the largest of the former Soviet republics. It was not a member of NATO, but for years it had been interested.

Ukraine had expressed its interest in joining NATO during the first part of the twenty-first century. By 2019, the country's membership aims were even written into its constitution. Early on, US president George W. Bush advocated for Ukraine's NATO membership.

NATO and Ukraine have discussed Ukrainian membership for more than a decade.

On April 3, 2008, the idea was formally recognized in the Bucharest Summit Declaration. "NATO welcomes Ukraine's and Georgia's Euro-Atlantic aspirations for membership in NATO," the statement read. "We agreed today that these countries will become members of NATO." There was no timeline specified. But the intentions were clear. Ukraine was a special friend to NATO and would eventually be part of the group.

Russia did not appreciate the encroach of new NATO members toward its borders. The country had shown it was willing to act without international approval to right perceived wrongs.

In 2014, Russia invaded a southern portion of Ukraine called Crimea and claimed it for Russia. Many other countries disapproved of the move. Putin seemed to view it as a homecoming. "Crimea has always been an integral part of Russia in the hearts and minds of people," he said at the time.

Putin felt similarly about Ukraine. In July 2021, he published an essay discussing the "historical unity" between the Russian and Ukrainian language, culture, and people.

US president George W. Bush and US secretary of state Condoleezza Rice at the 2008 NATO summit in Bucharest, Romania

In November 2021, Ukraine said Russia had stationed about 100,000 troops on their shared border. Satellite images confirmed the troops' presence. In December, US president Joe Biden threatened to enact sanctions against Russia if it attacked Ukraine. Russia asked that NATO agree not to make Ukraine or other former Soviet republics NATO members in the future.

Russian deputy foreign minister Sergei Ryabkov met with a US official in Geneva, Switzerland, on January 10, 2022. "For us, it's absolutely mandatory to make sure that Ukraine never, never, ever becomes a member of NATO," Ryabkov said. "We do not trust the other side."

NATO countries countered that the treaty allowed any interested European country that met certain standards a chance at membership. They said they would not close this door on Ukraine. At the same time, there was little evidence that Ukraine was poised to join NATO. Prospective members must be assigned a membership action plan. The plan describes reforms they will make to coordinate with NATO goals. Ukraine did not have such a plan.

By February 15, about 130,000 Russian troops lined Ukraine. The United States said it had learned a Russian invasion of Ukraine was planned to begin shortly. On Thursday, February 24, Russian troops entered Ukraine.

Russian military vehicles travel on a Crimean highway on January 18, 2022.

Zelenskyy, over video conference from Kyiv, converses with NATO leaders in Brussels on March 24.

CHAPTER TEN

TO BE OR NOT TO BE . . . INVOLVED

Russian troops quickly moved into Ukrainian territory. The port city of Mariupol became an area of intense combat and widespread destruction. Millions of refugees left the country to find safety. Some called for NATO and the US to provide military assistance for Ukraine. Others thought doing so would risk worsening the conflict.

Ukrainian president Volodymyr Zelenskyy asked the US and NATO multiple times to enforce a no-fly zone over Ukraine. Russian air forces were hitting Ukrainian cities with bombs. If the West created a no-fly zone, it would agree to shoot Russian aircraft down if the planes entered Ukrainian airspace.

On March 28, NATO issued a statement saying it "condemns in the strongest possible terms Russia's full-scale invasion of Ukraine." But it also said it would not enforce a no-fly zone because that "would bring NATO forces into direct conflict with Russia. This would significantly escalate the war and lead to more human suffering and destruction for all countries involved." US president Biden made similar statements. He added that the US would not engage directly with Russia unless Russia attacked a NATO member country.

The potential risk of direct NATO fighting with Russian forces became clear in February. Putin announced that he had put his nuclear weapons on high alert. He said this was a reaction to economic sanctions from the US and other countries. An implied nuclear threat like this was unusual, even by Cold War standards.

NATO has had varying levels of involvement in other world crises. This made the choice of "how much involvement" in the Ukraine crisis unclear. After the 9/11 terrorist attacks, the US and other Western

NEW MEMBERS

Sweden and Finland each applied for NATO membership on May 18, 2022, almost three months after the Russian invasion of Ukraine began. The US quickly expressed its support for the applications. Some suspected the process would take time. Approval of new members must be unanimous.

Secretary General Jens Stoltenberg said NATO would find ways to help Ukraine without sparking more violence.

countries entered Afghanistan. NATO itself was not formally involved until it took control of the ISAF for the stabilization process. Kosovo was not a NATO member. But NATO did carry out air raids to drive Serbian forces to retreat.

In Ukraine, experts thought direct NATO military involvement was unlikely. This was due to the risk of escalation and the need for agreement among all NATO members before action was taken. However, the alliance said it supported Ukraine in other ways.

NATO had 30 member countries in May 2022. Montenegro joined in 2017, and North Macedonia in 2020.

CHAPTER ELEVEN

SUPPORT FROM A DISTANCE

As the crisis unfolded, NATO acted in support of Ukraine. But it stopped short of direct military involvement. Implementing economic sanctions, lending weapons to Ukrainian forces, and negotiating on Ukraine's behalf were among the group's support activities. The crisis highlighted NATO's identity as a peacekeeping and defensive alliance. NATO minimized the military participation track the group developed in the early twenty-first century.

NATO repeatedly denied requests from Zelenskyy, Polish officials, and others to create a no-fly zone over the country. But the organization said it supported Ukraine's cause in many other, less direct ways.

In an NBC News interview, NATO secretary general Jens Stoltenberg described these activities. "NATO allies are stepping up their support to Ukraine, partly by delivering military support, humanitarian support, and billions of financial support to Ukraine," he said. "And then of course we also imposed unprecedented sanctions on Russia to make sure President Putin is paying a high price for this totally unjustified, senseless war." In its March 28 statement, NATO did not provide immediate details on the sanctions. But it said they were "massive and severe."

Secretary General Stoltenberg promised additional aid to Ukraine at a meeting in Brussels on March 24. The full aid package was not expected to come until June. NATO promised to send four "battlegroups" to Bulgaria, Hungary, Romania, and Slovakia. Four other groups were already stationed in nearby countries, including

ECONOMIC SANCTIONS ON RUSSIA

A cascade of economic restrictions against Russia followed the country's February 24 invasion of Ukraine, many of them from NATO members. On April 6, the US announced it froze transactions with Russia's largest bank and would forbid new investment in Russia. The European Union earlier said it would limit exports of high-tech items to Russia.

The US figured Russia's economy would shrink up to 15 percent in 2022. It also said more than 600 companies stopped doing business in Russia.

Poland. NATO also planned to help Ukraine with cybersecurity and humanitarian efforts.

The crisis in Ukraine tested NATO's cohesion. It forced it to define when and to whom it would provide support. In its more than 70 years, NATO had changed. It evolved from a defensive pact to a spreader of Western European values. It would later become a platform for targeted military operations in the name of peace.

The treaty organization would likely continue to reposition itself in world affairs. But at the time of the Ukraine crisis, NATO emphasized that its actions "are defensive, designed not to provoke a conflict but to prevent a conflict."

NATO leadership pledged to send battlegroups to four Eastern European countries.

TIMELINE OF NATO

In its more than 73 years, NATO has grown from a collective defense treaty among 12 nations into an active Western alliance 30 countries strong.

APRIL 4, 1949
Twelve nations sign the North Atlantic Treaty in Washington, DC.

1955
The Warsaw Pact is signed in Poland on May 14; West Germany joins NATO.

1961
The Berlin Wall is built to separate East and West Berlin.

1952
The Supreme Headquarters Allied Powers Europe (SHAPE) is established in Paris; Greece and Turkey join NATO.

1956
Soviet forces defeat uprisings in Hungary and Poland.

1987
Soviet premier Mikhail Gorbachev and US president Ronald Reagan sign the Intermediate-Range Nuclear Forces Treaty.

DECEMBER 25, 1991
Gorbachev resigns, signaling the end of the Soviet Union.

2003
NATO takes over control of the International Security Assistance Force (ISAF) in Afghanistan.

NOVEMBER 9, 1989
The Berlin Wall falls.

1999
Poland, Hungary, and the Czech Republic join NATO; Serbian forces withdraw from Kosovo and NATO troops enter to secure peace.

1966
France announces it will leave NATO's military arm.

1968
The Brezhnev Doctrine is announced.

1983
NATO begins to deploy Pershing II missiles.

1966

1968

1983

1967

1979

1967
The SHAPE moves from Paris to Brussels, Belgium; in December, the Harmel Report is released.

DECEMBER 24, 1979
The Soviet Union takes control of Afghanistan to stabilize communist rule there.

JUNE 2017
Ukraine passes a law saying it will aim for NATO membership.

FEBRUARY 24, 2022
Russia invades Ukraine.

2017

2022

2008

2021

2022

APRIL 3, 2008
The Bucharest Summit Declaration recognizes Ukraine's hopes to be a NATO member in the future.

NOVEMBER 2021
Russia stations about 100,000 troops along its border with Ukraine.

MARCH 24, 2022
At a special meeting, NATO pledges to help Ukraine with humanitarian and other efforts but stops short of enforcing a no-fly zone over the country.

GLOSSARY

administration – the people who manage a presidential government.

advocate – to take action in support of something.

blockade – the cutting off of an area by soldiers or ships.

capitalism – an economic system where businesses compete to sell their products and services.

civilian – of or relating to something nonmilitary.

Cold War – a period of tension and hostility between the United States and its allies and the Soviet Union and its allies after World War II.

communism – a social and economic system in which everything is owned by the government and given to the people as needed. A person who believes in communism is called a communist.

complementary – relating to things that go well together.

democracy – a governmental system in which the people vote on how to run their country.

détente – a relaxing of tense relations.

dictator – a ruler with complete control who often governs cruelly.

diplomacy – the practice of handling discussions and compromises between nations.

doctrine – a set of beliefs or a policy.

entrenched – existing for a long time; established.

escalate – to increase in intensity or extent.

ethnic cleansing – the removal of one cultural group by another by exiling, imprisoning, or killing.

maneuver – a clever or skillful move or plan.

nationalism – a belief that one's country is better than all others.

no-fly zone – where military planes are forbidden to fly during war.

obsolete – no longer relevant or useful.

sanction – an action by several nations against another nation to force it to obey an international law.

satellite – a country controlled by a more powerful country.

socialism – a type of economic or political system where either the government or all the citizens control the production and distribution of goods. The terms *communism* and *socialism* are sometimes used interchangeably.

INDEX

A
Afghanistan, 31-32, 43, 55

B
Berlin Wall, 23, 36
Biden, Joe, 50, 54
Brezhnev, Leonid, 29
Brezhnev Doctrine, 29, 35-36

C
capitalism, 5, 12, 39
Cold War, 5-6, 8, 17, 19, 23, 31-33, 35-38, 41, 43, 47, 54
collective defense, 12, 16, 19, 25, 45
communism, 5-6, 11-12, 17, 20, 29, 31-32, 35-36

D
democracy, 5-6, 31
détente, 28, 31-32

E
Eisenhower, Dwight D., 15-16, 22-23

F
"flexible response" policy, 25

G
Gorbachev, Mikhail, 33, 35-37

H
Harmel, Pierre, 28

I
International Security Assistance Force (ISAF), 43, 54
Ismay, Lord Hastings Lionel, 16

K
Kennedy, John F., 25, 32
Kosovo, 42, 55

M
massive retaliation, 16, 25
membership, 5-7, 16, 27, 36, 39, 44-45, 47-48, 50, 54
missiles, 31-33

N
no-fly zone, 53-54, 57

P
Poroshenko, Petro, 6
Putin, Vladimir, 47, 49, 54, 58

R
Reagan, Ronald, 33, 36
Russia, 5, 7, 11, 20, 43, 47-50, 53-54, 58

S
sanctions, 50, 54, 57-58
Stoltenberg, Jens, 57-58
Supreme Headquarters Allied Powers Europe (SHAPE), 15, 26

T
targeted military operations, 8, 41-43, 59

U
Ukraine, 5-8, 47-50, 53-55, 57-59
Union of Soviet Socialist Republics (USSR), 5, 8, 11-13, 17, 19-20, 23, 25-26, 29, 31-33, 35, 37-38
United Nations, 42
United States (US), 12, 15, 22, 25, 32-33, 35, 43, 47, 50, 53-54

W
Warsaw Pact, 19-20, 37
World War II, 8, 11-12, 15, 25

Z
Zelenskyy, Volodymyr, 53, 57